TAMMI MOORE

The Little Book Of Empowering Words

A Small Collection of Positive Affirmations To Speak Throughout The Day

D1713825

"What you're supposed to do when you don't like a thing is change it. If you can't change it, change the way you think about it. Don't complain."

— MAYA ANGELOU, WOULDN'T TAKE NOTHING FOR MY JOURNEY NOW

Contents

1

Introduction

Greetings and welcome to the "Little Book of Empowering Words". My name is Tammi Moore and I am delighted to share with you, a small condensed collection of uplifting and inspiring affirmations that I have found to be useful in my daily life. Whether I'm feeling anxious, insecure, doubtful, discouraged or just plain "not feeling it", the empowering words that I am about to share with you, have made a major shift in my life, for the good. Through my practice, I have gone from worrying that I'm not enough, second-guessing myself and my abilities, and feelings of hopelessness, to a new transforming and empowering belief – that there is uplifting power in spoken words to change what I believe about myself and what I can accomplish.

I came across the idea to compile a short list of empowering and inspiring affirmations for people on the go, sort of like a "pocket guide", where you can access it when you need some encouraging or uplifting words to embolden you to feel that can live your best life. I remember how I sometimes needed those optimistic words to get me through a stressful situation or inspire my creativity or elevate my confidence.

And for the life of me, I couldn't remember those exact words that had motivated me from previous times. Hence, the "Little Book of Empowering Words", now at my fingertips. I like having them in one space, available when I need them. Instead of trying to recall them.

I'm sure at some point we have come across an inspirational quote or phrase that sat well with us and stimulated us to continue and not give up. You know those illuminating words that rang out and settled deep in our core. I'm referring to those thought-provoking words that changed our perspective on how we view ourselves and the world. How about those endearing words that loosened the cords of our heart, allowing the free flow of tears. Whatever the experience may have been, empowering words most likely left you feeling inspired, encouraged, energized and electrified, more confident, motivated, calm. For that is what affirmations are designed to do. The very word itself is defined as "positive statements or phrases" that put to test the negative or unhelpful thoughts". So when you are repeatedly saying positive words or phrases, the negative thoughts are unable to hang around. For some reason, that is either known or unknown, we seem to easily gravitate towards the negative. Perhaps, it's the constant negative streams of information that we are bombarded with on a daily basis. Whether we are aware or unaware of the impact of negative words, our body and mind absorbs them. And just the simple reassuring word, can change our demeanor, our outlook. And if that is the case, then making a conscious effort to speak admiringly or emphatically about oneself, makes life a little better and is worth the practice. Wouldn't you agree?

There is compelling research and theory that if positive affirming words are practiced consistently and repeatedly, our brain will attempt to automatically think these thoughts. (Paulhus & Coue, 1993). Furthermore, there is additional research available that says, WE have the ability to

CHANGE the way we THINK of ourselves. (Demarin & Morovic, 2014). How amazing our brain is! We are indeed fascinating and divine beings. We just need to tap into ourselves to see the beauty that already exists.

This book isn't necessarily read from cover to cover. Rather, if there is a chapter in the table of contents that resonates with you, then you can go directly to that chapter. For instance, maybe you're about to give a talk on what you're passionate about, in front of a large audience, and start to feel some self doubt. This is a good time to reach for your Little Book of Empowering Words to the section on "Dealing with Difficult Situations". There you may find just the right affirmative words to encourage and empower you. Or another example, would be the section on Cultivating Good Thoughts for a Restful Sleep if you're having difficulty shutting down the chatter in your brain. Sleep is vitally important for our brains to process all the information and memories that we have accumulated in a day. Speaking purposeful and soothing words can aid in creating a quiet and peaceful environment for restful sleep and our brain can do it's business.

There are numerous ways to use this little book to generate more ease of mind, boost your courage, invigorate your creativity, rouse your happiness and intensify the love in your life. I personally like to start my day with confident and uplifting words to set the tone for the morning. It has a way of bringing out the best part of me, that I sometimes forget about. This can be part of your morning practice. And the same when ending your day. Or maybe you just need a gentle reminder of how amazing you are as a person. Oh, don't forget the encouragement and celebration on how far you've come to reaching a goal. Explore different chapters even if you think it may not pertain to you.

If you've never practiced saying affirmations, I discovered some quick tips, that may be helpful, on getting started.

1. **Speak out loud, your empowering words.** Use your voice, even if it's just a whisper. This is strategic in getting your other senses involved. Like hearing and feeling. When speaking out loud or even whispering, you can hear and feel the words coming out of your mouth. You may want to add calming meditative music while speaking your words.

2. **Say your affirming words in the present tense**, not in the past or not in the future. Say it in the now.

For example, you can say "I am a kind person", instead of "I can be a kind person". By saying "I am", your attention is now on transforming your beliefs about yourself in the present moment, instead of trying to set a goal for the future. I will be sharing a lot of "I am" in the affirmations, so you can connect and let the focus be on you.

3. **Choose only those empowering words that really matter and are important to you**, so that you'll stay committed in your practice. If something doesn't sound right or doesn't flow right, it's most likely because it's new to your ears and your brain is adjusting to a new thought, a positive one. Feel free to change it up to what sounds and feels right for you. Perhaps you will come up with your own empowering words.

4. **Repeat, Repeat, Repeat** those empowering phrases 5-10 times slowly or as many times as you need to, so that you believe and absorb every word. Practice up to 3-5 times daily to reinforce the positive thoughts. Our brains are a miraculous gift that learns new thoughts and releases old thoughts that don't align with us anymore. If this is new to you, be kind to yourself. Allow this practice to be a sacred private

moment that you can come to as often as you like.

5. **See yourself.** If possible, I encourage you to stand in front of a mirror when repeating your phrases. It's one way of connecting with yourself. Although it may seem awkward at first, after a while don't be surprised if the tears begin to flow.

I invite you to take a journey into the Little Book of Empowering Words.

Let's begin...

2

Grateful And Inspiring Affirmations To Wake Up To

"Yesterday is history, tomorrow is a mystery, today is a gift of God, which is why we call it the present."
— *Bill Keane*

Mornings have become my favorite part of the day. I am blessed to be able to see the rising sun come over the distant mountain landscape. It awakens my soul to a new day. As the sun rays shine and ripple like water through the gentle wind blown tree that sits in my front yard. And then filters through the partially open slats of my shutters, bringing the warmth and tender brightness of a new day. I smile with delight that I am present for this moment.

When I wake up in the morning, I am grateful for the opening of my eyes and the moving of my body and the sounds that I sometimes take for granted. Like the singing of the birds outside my home office window and the warm running water flowing from the faucet that washes my face. And I'm thinking, what empowering words will I speak today, to set the tone, to move the needle. Morning gives us an opportunity to start over on a clean slate. No matter what happened yesterday, good or bad, right or wrong. We can't go back, we can only be here in the present. What will you do today that is radically different from yesterday? I'm sure you know of someone who is "positively perky" or has that morning energetic vibe. I sometimes used to wonder, how do they do that, is it possible for me? It is. Perhaps they are saying these:

- *"I am awake, alive and breathing, all good things await me!"*
- *"I am grateful to be awakened to a new day, new beginnings, new possibilities."*
- *"I choose to be happy today"*

- *"I am excited to make a positive impact in someone's life today"*
- *"I am deserving of good things and success"*
- *"I am forgiving, I am letting go"*
- *"Today is going to be full of positivity, I get to choose"*
- *" I am here, the world is waiting for me"*
- *"I am living for today!"*

3

Workplace Affirmations For Resilience

"*S*uccess is not final, failure is not fatal: it is the courage to continue that counts."
— **Winston S. Churchill**

There are times, when the workplace environment, can be challenging, to say the least. And there are times when you don't feel you are at the top of your "A" game or maybe you're feeling a little "burnout". Maybe there is an approaching deadline on a project and feelings of anxiousness are coming about and you're thinking, "I'm not going to make it". Perhaps you are dreading the constant complaints or negative comments from a coworker that seep into your world and attempt to steal your joy. Whatever the case may be, there are situations and occurrences that are out of our control. But, be encouraged, that we all have the ability to speak positivity into our own hearts and minds. Giving us a mindful place of refuge and peace and encouragement. Take a moment, take a breath and try these affirming words:

- *"I am in control of my emotions and I choose to be calm and at peace"* (*take a breath*)
- *"I am willing and capable of learning new things"*
- *"My positive words have value and worth"*
- *"I learn and grow from my failures"*
- *" I am creative and confident in my unique talents"*
- *"I'm doing the best I can at this moment, and that is enough."* (*take a breath*)
- *"I am a valuable and important"*
- *"I am going to get through this, one breath, one step at a time"*

4

Affirmations For Work/Life Balance

"Two roads diverged in a wood, and I -I took the one less traveled by,
And that has made all the difference."
— *Robert Frost*

There seems to be an ongoing struggle in our minds, that if we are not working constantly, then we are not being productive. We tend to wear many hats. The high achiever, the go-getter, the over-timer, the go-to-person, the problem solver, the caregiver of the world. Perhaps we have learned that keeping busy and doing the "busy-ness" is what is expected of us to be successful. Although these roles are not inherently bad, they may not be sustainable. For we will soon tire out. Something or someone will be forgotten about. And that someone is usually ourselves. The programming from society or our upbringing has often made us believe that we must take care of others first and if there's time we can tend to our own weary worn out needs. Which doesn't always happen often enough. Because we're always waiting for time. If I could have one more hour in a day, then I can… We'll mostly likely fill that extra hour doing for others.

In order for us to live a more balanced life between work and home and the world, perhaps we should tell ourselves that we are only human. Human, in the sense that we are not robotic without feeling or emotion. We, indeed, have tender feelings that need nurtured. Emotional and heart-felt pain that needs to be acknowledged. A need for belonging and being connected to others. Realizing all of this, it is appropriate that we give ourselves permission to have moments of kindness, love and care for ourselves (self-care) or just simply sit with your thoughts and feelings and… do nothing… and be at peace and be aware and be grateful that you took the time to be human. In those moments, you will be refreshed in your mind, body and soul, making you a more balanced and productive person. For we only have one body that is our own. Care deeply… I invite you to practice these empowering words and be the caretaker of you:

- *"I am hardworking, I give myself permission to rest"*
- *"I love making time for me and me alone"*

14

- *"The more I fill my cup, the more I have to give"*
- *"I am able to say, "No" and be okay with it"*
- *"Today, I am slowing down and being present"*
- *"I am deserving of me-time"*
- *"I am loving myself today, so I can love others"*
- *"I am making time to care for me today"*
- *"I am only human, I am just one person"*
- *"I am learning to make myself a priority"*

5

Encouraging Affirmations For Men

"Don't judge each day by the harvest you reap but by the seeds that you plant."
— *Robert Louis Stevenson*

I believe sometimes we forget that our men need support too. Daily demands and high expectations, most often, leave our men feeling burdened and undervalued.

It may seem like the weight of the world is laying on your shoulders, and you may be thinking it is my duty, my obligation as a man to fulfill it all, so that my loved ones look up to me as being capable and a strong pillar. Those daily pressures of taking care of your family, ensuring that they have everything needed are often unappreciated or taken for granted. Maybe you're thinking I have to be all and know all, to be a good father or husband or son. And now you're feeling overwhelmed or unworthy of responsibilities or unsure that you have what it takes. Or maybe, you're not sure how to show your true feelings and emotions, because you were taught that showing your feelings or emotions was a weakness. Society sometimes leaves us with little to no space for just being a person trying to figure it all out in our own time... a space to just be you.. a man. I can tell you that grown men cry. My father was an excellent provider for our family. The efficient handyman and remodeler, the green-thumb lawn and gardener, the hunter and the fisherman and I thought he could fix or do anything, that he was strong as an ox and gently fearsome. And then I saw for the first time, as a teenager, the raw emotions of a man that felt pain in his heart for a loved one that died unexpectedly and tragically. A steady stream of tears that rolled down his cheekbone, let me know that my dad had feelings too. And that grown strong and fearsome men cry. I invite you to take this time and try these:

- *"I am living the part of a son/brother/husband/father respectfully and caringly"*
- *"I am a man, I am allowed to feel, I am allowed to cry"*
- *"I am strong and capable of expressing my emotions"*
- *"I am ready to face new challenges"*
- *"I am growing and learning everyday"*
- *"I choose to surround myself with positive people"*

- *"I am a good person and I have worth"*
- *"I am doing my very best and that means everything"*
- *"I am a father/son/husband/brother and I am a blessing"*
- *"I am true to myself, I am a man"*
- *"I have what it takes to be a dad/husband"*
- *"I am a man in progress, growing and learning daily"*
- *"I am learning to love myself"*
- *"I am planting good seeds in my life"*

6

Empowering Affirmations For Women

"I f you have good thoughts they will shine out of your face like sunbeams and you will always look lovely."
— *Roald Dahl*

Society has had a huge impact on how we perceive ourselves as women. The idea that we only fit one mold, should never be. For we are divinely created and unique in every way. Our shapes, our sizes, our array of color, our voices and the way we carry ourselves, are all exclusive and unmatched. Sometimes we often think that we are less than perfect and always need fixing. But to the contrary, for we are an extraordinary creation and we are not broken. We are blooming daughters, nurturing mothers, doting grandmothers, inspiring aunties, loving sisters and courageous women. I believe all women everywhere need to be reminded of how essential they are to people in their lives, and also to the entire world. For all the tender hugs, kissed skinned knees, warm smiles of encouragement, hands held, tears wiped away, the I-love-you's and have-a-good-day, a listening ear to confide in, I'm-standing-by-you and with-you and so much more. You have loved many and are loved by many. Allow these affirmations to transform your thinking.

- *"I am beautiful, inside and out"*
- *"I love myself, just as I am"*
- *"I am and have always been enough"*
- *"I am grateful, for my body is unique and lovely"*
- *"I am naturally nurturing and loving"*
- *"I am strong and capable"*
- *"I am a daughter/mother/sister/wife and I am still me...a woman"*
- *"I am touching many lives in a positive and unforgetful way"*

- *"I am caring for my body and my mind"*
- *"I am worth being loved"*
- *"I have purpose, I am needed"*

7

Inspiring Affirmations For Kids Of All Ages

"You is kind. You is smart. You is important."
— *Kathryn Stockett, The Help*

When I was kid, I can remember growing up and wondering how I fit into this world. I had feelings of uncertainty about understanding and knowing everything. I used to think, "will I grow up to be good enough", "will my parents be proud of me, even if I fail". "Will I be accepted by my friends, for I only want to just fit in and belong". "Am I beautiful". These are just a few of the thoughts that went through my head as a kid. The thoughts I had developed about myself and carried into adulthood, determined what kind of action I would take or not take... what decisions I would make or not make...and what I thought I could be or wasn't capable of being. And because of those thoughts, I have a special place in my heart for kids, especially those who don't realize the grand possibilities that they possess to go out in the world and be great. We are sometimes unaware that children from an early age are absorbing everything that they hear and see around them at a rapid rate. There is so much information that is being programmed into the developing clean slate of their brains. Whether it is positivity for growth that builds and uplifts or negativity that may do the opposite. And that is why I believe that kids should be seen as individuals, unique and their own person. Their voices should be heard to express and form their opinions. Their feelings and thoughts should be acknowledged and valued. And most importantly, kids should be told that they are loved, unconditionally and told they are beautiful, immeasurably. If you are a kid or a kid at heart, I invite you to empower yourself with affirmative words. It is humanly possible that you can change the way you feel and the way you think about yourself. Practice saying the phrases below in front of a mirror. It makes a difference.

Help a kid with these affirming words:

- *"I am my own person, I am me"*
- *"I am beautiful"*

- *"I am loved"*
- *"I love me"*
- *"My mistakes are okay, I am learning and growing"*
- *"I believe in me"*
- *"I like me, just the way I am"*
- *"I have an amazing brain, I can learn new things"*
- *"I belong in this world"*
- *"I have a voice, I can express myself"*
- *"My feelings matter"*
- *"I have an opinion"*
- *"My life has value and worth"*
- *"I choose to make good choices today"*
- *"I see me, I hear me, I love you me"* (repeat to yourself in front of a mirror)

8

Motivational Affirmations For Optimal Health/Fitness

"I never said it would be easy, I only said it would be worth it."
— *Mae West*

I was once told that motivation is not really reliable, that it's not always dependable. And there may be some truth to that. Because if you're not feeling it, obviously motivation is not working so much. But then I learned that there is power in the words that you speak to yourself. For example, if you wake up in the morning and you planned to go to the gym or workout at home before you start your day. Your mind may be telling you, "I really don't feel like it today, maybe tomorrow". But what if your mind tells your body, "it's time to get up and go beautiful!, because you know your stunning body will thank you and you'll feel boundlessly energized". Chances are you will get up and go work out and feel absolutely fabulous in both your body and your mind, because of positive affirmations that you spoke. You spoke tender, endearing, kind and uplifting words that can change the course of the moment. I believe that with consistency, we can program our minds to be motivational, to be inspired, to want good health and well being.

Many of us, myself included, have struggled with food choices. We are informed and we know pretty much what is healthy and what is not. But sometimes we can make being healthy so complicated and it doesn't have to be. We eat a certain way because we believe that it's healthy and we may obsess over it. We sometimes believe that no pain, no gain. And we may find ourselves obsessing over that too. And then when we don't follow through, or we mess up and lose our way, or we don't see the results we're looking for, we become demotivated. We can always get back on track. But what will keep us there... What will be our staying power? Perhaps a bolstering word would change the way we feel about it or the way we envision ourselves. When motivation seems to be needing a gentle reminder of your vision, then try these empowering words:

- *"I am staying the course to be healthy"*
- *"I am not giving up, even if it's hard"*
- *"I am doing this, I have the power to move"*
- *"I know and feel changes are happening, even if I can't see it yet"*
- *"Nothing will get in the way of my success"*
- *"I am making good choices for my health"*
- *"I celebrate all my little wins, I am making progress"*
- *"I am doing this for me"*
- *"I am eating for energy"*
- *"I am releasing guilt and shame"*
- *"I am a champion in this thing called healthy"*

9

Affirmations For Spiritual Gratitude

"More smiling, less worrying. More compassion, less judgment. More blessed, less stressed. More love, less hate."
— *Roy T. Bennett, The Light in the Heart*

When it comes to spirituality, I have found in my own practice that connecting to the Creator with liberating words, has elevated my meditation experience and increased my awareness of how our minds are beautiful and intricate. It is indeed a free spiritual awakening and connection that can deepen your spiritual walk and release the chains that keep us bound.

We have been blessed with the ability to activate the breath to calm our beings. And with that calmness, we are able to usher in the other senses and visualize in our minds who we are now and what we envision ourselves to be. With the sense of hearing, we are able to absorb the sound of our voices speaking confident and loving words, thereby nurturing our souls.

As I was referencing the Bible, I came across an encouraging letter written by Paul (Shaul) to encourage a group of believers in Philippi to - think on these things... Whatever is true, noble, righteous, pure, lovely, admirable, excellent and praiseworthy. I believe he was trying to encourage them to think positively in spite of their circumstances. And all of this... produces gratitude in my heart for what I am able to do freely...speak empowering words and subsequently feel and think graciously.

I invite you to practice gratitude every day, for it has a way of bringing a smile into your heart, regardless of your circumstances.

- *"I am an amazing creation, I am my own unique person"*
- *"I am blessed with good thoughts and kind words"*
- *"I have compassion for myself and others"*
- *"I am smiling in my heart, I am at peace"*
- *"I am trusting the Creator is guiding me in every way "*
- *"I am not alone"*

- *"My life has purpose, I am here and I am needed"*
- *"I radiate positive energy to the world"*
- *"I am exactly who and where I'm supposed to be"*
- *"I am thankful for everything great and small"*
- *"I am thinking on good things"*

10

Ending The Day With Thoughtful Affirming Words

A t the end of the day, let there be no excuses, no explanations, no regrets."

— Steve Maraboli, Life, the Truth, and Being Free

Allow yourself a little time before bed or sleep to reflect upon the day. Maybe it was hectic or stressful in some way. Maybe you didn't think you had enough time to complete something or say something. Maybe you're thinking I could have done better. Now shift your reflection on something else… the positive's, the blessings, the gratitudes, the fulfilling moments, the big and small wins, the random acts of kindness, and the love that you gave or received. If nothing is coming up, think lightly on simple things we take for granted like a smile to a stranger, a thank you, a wave hello or goodbye, a hug, a kind word. All of these and many more are undeniable feedback and empowering events that are able to connect us with others and even ourselves. Filling up our hearts and minds with overwhelming gratitude. Focus on those moments and speak empowering words. Good night and sleep well:

- *"I am rejoicing for all the kind moments today"*
- *"I made it, I am well"*
- *"I am grateful for my life"*
- *"My day was sweet and filled with blessings"*
- *"I am at peace and at home in my body"*
- *"I am ending my day with gratitude and joy"*
- *"I choose to forgive and let go"*
- *"I am going to sleep with peace and stillness in my heart"*
- *"My body, my mind, my soul are safe to rest"*
- *"I am releasing my negative thoughts, and choosing calmness and peace"*

11

Conclusion

Empowering words no matter how small or seemingly insignificant, can impact our lives greatly. The words that we hear everyday, whether positive or negative, will either lift you up or tear you down. What is so profound is that we ourselves have the ability to speak resolute words and change our thoughts to produce immense outcomes. It is our choice.

There is an interesting acronym I discovered on my journey, called T.F.A.R.- Think. Feel. Action. Results. The concept behind it is that what you think leads to your feelings, your feelings lead to actions and your actions lead to results. So imagine, if you implemented speaking positively to yourself, and your negative thoughts were overcome with empowering words that lead you to take action on something you previously believed was not possible for you. And as a result of your actions, you were able to live your best life! Glorious!

The many benefits of consistently speaking empowering words has been known to be supportive when dealing with periods of anxiousness, fear, lack of motivation, low self esteem or lack of confidence. It allows a person to be more resilient when faced with difficulties, which can then lead to a better outcome. Furthermore, affirmations lead us to be more optimistic about our life and our circumstances. Consider incorporating empowering words with any existing therapy prescribed by your physician or therapist.

Some may believe that affirmations are self-centered. But on the contrary, the Biblical Scriptures even tell us to love our neighbors as ourselves. For when we truly love and care for ourselves, then we can effectively love and care for others.

There is some truth behind the phrase "you are what you think". When we begin to say the affirmative words, and then we start to think confidently and before you know it...we are what we think...beautiful, creative, loving, adventurous, daring, charming, kind, compassionate, forgiving, courageous, fearless, confident, calm, resilient, happy and free to be...

It was my hope that this little book of empowering words exhilarated you in great and lasting ways. That you could simply speak a phrase of uplifting words and change the trajectory of your morning, your afternoon, your evening and even your life. That a few simple igniting words would uplift sadness, inspire creativity, spark enthusiasm and bolster courage so that you may dream endlessly, love genuinely and live courageously.

No, we may not be able to change the world around us, but we are able to change how we think of ourselves and how we respond to the world.

I hope you enjoyed this little book as much as I enjoyed writing it. And if you found this book helpful and supportive, I'd be very appreciative if you left a favorable review on Amazon. Thank you.

May you keep this in your heart and mind, and know that those heartfelt empowering words were always there and just needed to be simply spoken.

❤Warmly,
   Tammi

12

Resources

M. (2022, June 5). *List Of Affirmations - 90 Great Words Of Affirmations List*. Mindbless. https://mindbless.com/list-of-affirmations/

Daily Affirmations: Definition, Benefits, & 102 Examples to Improve Your Life. (n.d.). The Berkeley Well-Being Institute. https://www.berkeleywellbeing.com/daily-affirmations.html

Utterly Positive. (2023, February 14). *All Lists Of Affirmations: 2500+ Positive Affirmations For Everyday*. https://utterlypositive.com/lists-of-affirmations/

Inspirational Quotes (68122 quotes). (n.d.). https://www.goodreads.com/quotes/tag/inspirational

Moore, C. P. (2023, February 25). *Positive Daily Affirmations: Is There Science Behind It?* PositivePsychology.com. https://positivepsychology.

com/daily-affirmations/

Lannon, R. (2007, December 5). *Be Prepared to Change Your Thinking T.F.A.R. Think, Feel Act Results.* ezarticles.com. Retrieved March 5, 2023, from https://ezinearticles.com/?Be-Prepared-To-Change-Your-Think ing—-T.F.A.R.—-Think,-Feel,-Act,-Results!&id=867335

About the Author

Tammi is a seasoned nurse, mindfulness health coach and aspiring writer who was born in the nation's capitol, Washington D.C., raised in the rolling hills of Pennsylvania and has lived in Illinois and Colorado. During her nursing career, Tammi developed a love and passion for serving and empowering people on their journey back to health and wellness. She continues to nurture her passion by learning, implementing and sharing with others, all the natural and holistic ways to heal your body, mind and soul.

Tammi is currently operating her health coaching business, journey2health.tammi LLC, from her home in Arizona where she resides with her constant companion, loving and devoted husband, Michael. They have 5 extraordinary and remarkable children. In her free time, Tammi enjoys family time, traveling, the great outdoors, documentaries, reading and journaling.

You can connect with me on:

🌐 https://www.journey2healthtammi.com

Made in the USA
Middletown, DE
25 March 2023

27672923R00029